Forces & Motion

PETER RILEY

Heinemann Library
Des Plaines, Illinois

Designed by AMR
Illustrations by Art Construction and Jon Davis
Printed in Hong Kong

04 03 02 01 00
10 9 8 7 6 5 4 3 2 1

Library of Congress Cataloging-in-Publication Data

Riley, Peter D.
    Forces & motion / Peter Riley.
        p. cm. – (Science topics)
    Includes bibliographical references and index.
    Summary: Discusses various aspects of force and motion, including
gravity, the measurement of forces, Newton's laws, speed, friction,
air resistance, floating and sinking, magnetic force, and
electricity.
    ISBN 1-57572-772-2 (lib. bdg.)
    1. Force and energy Juvenile literature. 2. Motion Juvenile
literature. [1. Force and energy. 2. Motion.] I. Title.
II. Title: Forces and motion. III. Series.
QC73.4.R49 1999
531'.6—dc21   99-12885
                                                        CIP

Acknowledgments
The Publishers would like to thank the following for permission to reproduce photographs:
Action Plus/Phillippe Millereau, p. 4; Science Photo Library/Jerry Lodriguss, p. 5; Science Photo
Library/Julian Baum, p. 6; J. Allan Cash, pp. 7, 17, 23 bottom, 27, 28; Frank Spooner Pictures/
Sydney Freelance, p. 9 top; FLPA/Lee Rue/Images of Nature, p. 9 bottom; Telegraph Colour
Library/FPG International, p. 11 top; Action Plus/Glyn Kirk, pp. 11 bottom, 16, 20; Frank
Spooner Pictures/Brock Peter/Liaison, p. 12; Frank Spooner Pictures/Burrow/Liaison, p. 13; Action
Plus/Chris Barry, p. 15 top; John Cleare/Mountain Camera, p. 15 bottom; The Stock
Market/Brownie Harris, pp. 18, 23 top; Action Plus/Richard Francis, p. 19; B & C Alexander,
p. 21; Science Photo Library/Martyn F. Chillmaid, p. 24; Science Photo Library/Alex Bartel,
p. 25; Science Photo Library/Bruce Iverson, p. 26; Science Photo Library; p. 29.

Cover photograph reproduced with permission of Action-Plus Photographic.

Our thanks to Jane Tylor for her comments in the preparation of this book.

Every effort has been made to contact copyright holders of any material reproduced in this book.
Any omissions will be rectified in subsequent printings if notice is given to the Publisher.

Any words appearing in the text in bold, **like this**, are explained in the Glossary.

Contents

What is a Force?

A **force** is a push or a pull that usually produces **motion** (movement). When something is in motion, it is moving. A force can make a stationary object start to move. It can make a moving object change direction, speed up, slow down, or stop. A force can also make an object change its shape.

How your body pushes and pulls

You can soon identify where forces act if you think about the movements you feel and see in your daily life. For example, the first force you may notice in the morning is the pull of the muscles on your eyelids. Other forces that follow may be the pulling forces of arm and leg muscles on your bones. The muscles make your arms push your body out of bed and make your legs push you up into a standing position. From then on, your body exerts pushing and pulling forces on all kinds of things as you wash, get dressed, have breakfast, and prepare for the rest of the day. Think about these forces when you get up tomorrow.

Weight—your personal force

Your body pushes down on the ground with a force called weight. This force is caused by the pull of gravity on the substances that make up your muscles, bones, brain, and other organs in your body.

The forces acting on these cars send them in different directions and change their shape!

Pairs of forces

When a force acts in one direction, there is a second force that acts in the opposite direction. This means that forces always act in pairs. When the strength of a force acting in one direction is matched by the strength of a force acting in the opposite direction, the forces are balanced and there is no movement. Just close this book and press on its front and back covers with each hand with the same force and the book will stay still. Now, push slightly harder with one hand and see how the book changes position. If the strength of one force changes, the forces no longer balance and movement takes place.

How still are you?

You may not think you are moving as you read these words, but your eye muscles will have pulled your eyes to the right and left as you read this sentence. Your **pulse** is throbbing at a rate of more than once per second in your wrists and neck as your heart beats inside your chest to push blood through your body.

Your whole body and surroundings are moving at more than 180 miles (290 kilometers) per hour as the earth spins on its axis. You are moving in other directions, too, because Earth is moving around the sun, and the sun and its planets are moving around the center of the **Milky Way** (our **galaxy**). The earth is pulled around the sun by the force of gravity. This same force pulls the **solar system** around the Milky Way. Nothing in the **universe** is still. Even the galaxies are moving apart. Scientists believe that this is the result of an explosion called the Big Bang that formed the universe 15 billion years ago. All of these movements in the universe, both large and small, take place because of the push or pull of a force.

▶ Thousands of millions of stars pulled by the force of gravity are moving around the center of this galaxy.

Gravity in the Universe

There is a **force** of attraction between any two objects in the **universe**. This force is called **gravity**. Its effects can only be seen or felt when one object is very large (like Earth) and the other object is very much smaller (like you), or if the two objects are both very large (like the sun and the earth). A very large object like the earth has a **gravitational field** around it. This is a region around the object where gravity pulls on other objects. We live in the earth's gravitational field and see and feel its effects every moment of our lives. There are gravitational fields around other large objects in the universe too, and some of them affect conditions on Earth.

SCIENCE ESSENTIALS

A force of attraction exists between any two objects in the universe. This force is called gravity.
Gravity weakens with increasing distance from a planet, **moon,** or **star**. It holds the planets in their **orbits** in the **solar system**, causes the **tides** in Earth's oceans, and holds light inside a **black hole**.

The strongest pull of gravity

When certain stars finish shining, they eventually collapse. If a star over three times more massive than the sun collapses, it forms an object with such a strong force of gravity that even light—the fastest thing in the universe—cannot escape. This object is called a black hole. Its strong force of gravity pulls material out of any nearby star.

Material from the star on the left has been pulled away by the gravitational pull of the black hole. The material swirls around the black hole before it is finally drawn into it.

How gravity weakens

As you move away from a large object like the earth, its gravitational pull becomes weaker. A fast-moving airplane flying 6 miles (10 kilometers) above the earth would be pulled back to Earth if its jet engine were switched off. But a fast-moving space shuttle flying at more than 600 miles (965 kilometers) above the earth would be pulled around the planet in a path called an orbit if its engines were off. A spacecraft further out in space could pass the earth without being pulled by Earth's force of gravity at all.

The grip of gravity

The sun is more than a million times bigger than the earth, and its strong force of gravity holds the planets in their orbits in the solar system. Most of the planets have at least one moon. A moon moves in orbit around a planet, and is pulled by the force of gravity that exists between them.

Sun, moon, and tides

Our moon's gravitational force pulls on the surface of Earth. This does not affect the land, but the pull on the oceans creates two bulges in the water on opposite sides of the planet. As the earth rotates, the bulges move across the ocean surfaces and create high and low tides on the seashore. Twice a month, the sun, earth, and moon are in line as the moon orbits the earth. At these times, the pull of the sun's gravity adds to the pull of the moon's gravity and causes larger than usual high and low tides called spring tides.

► The gravitational force between the moon and the earth will pull the water down this beach.

Measuring Forces

A **force** such as **gravity** can be measured with an elastic material. An elastic material can be stretched or squashed by a force, but it returns to its original shape and size when the force is removed. The metal in a wire or spring is an example of an elastic material. A scale uses a spring. When an object is put on the scale, the pull of gravity changes the spring's shape.

SCIENCE ESSENTIALS

An elastic material can be stretched or squashed with a force but can return to its original shape.
If an elastic material is pushed or pulled beyond its elastic limit, its shape is changed permanently.
Mass is the amount of matter in an object.
Weight is the force of a mass pushing down on the earth.
A **newton** meter is a device for measuring forces.

Why elastic springs back

When a force pushes or pulls on an elastic material, a strain force develops inside the material that acts in the opposite direction. If the pushing or pulling force is removed, the strain force pushes or pulls the material back into its original shape. An elastic material obeys Hooke's Law.

Hooke's Law

Robert Hooke was an English scientist who lived 300 years ago. He performed experiments on wires and springs. He found that when a mass was added to a wire, the weight of the mass pulled the wire so that it stretched a certain amount. Through further experiments, Hooke found that the wire or spring stretched in proportion to the mass hanging on it. His observations became known as Hooke's Law. This discovery allowed people to compare the weights of objects. For example, an object with a large weight stretched a wire or spring to a greater extent than an object with a small weight.

Hooke's Law: the object with the larger mass stretches the spring more than the object with the smaller mass.

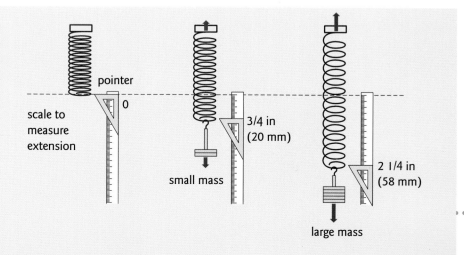

8

Measuring force

A newton meter is a device for measuring force. It contains a spring that can be stretched and a piece of metal to prevent it from being stretched beyond its elastic limit. A pointer is attached to the bottom of the spring. As the spring is stretched, the pointer moves over the scale.

When the stretching force is balanced by the strain force, the spring stops extending and the pointer shows the strength of the force on the scale. Forces are measured in units called newtons. When you peel a banana, you pull with a force of one newton.

◄ A newton meter could be used to measure the pulling force of this man as he pulls a jumbo jet more than 80 feet (24 meters) along a runway at Sydney Jet Base.

Change your planet to lose weight

Your mass is the amount of matter from which you are made. Your weight is the force with which you push down on the earth. This force is due to the pull of gravity between you and the earth. The force of gravity that exists between you and a planet depends on the size of the planet. Mars is smaller than Earth and the force of gravity in its **gravitational field** is only one-third that of Earth. This means that if you went to Mars, your weight would be one-third of the weight you are now! You would still be the same size because your mass would not have changed.

► The mass of this raccoon is squashing a spring inside the scale. A pointer attached to the spring has moved to show the raccoon's weight.

Getting Going

Sir Isaac Newton was a scientist who lived 300 years ago and studied the way objects move. From his studies, he stated three laws of **motion**. They describe how **forces** act and how objects behave when they are still or moving.

SCIENCE ESSENTIALS

Sir Isaac Newton stated three laws of motion. They explain why things stay still or move.
An unbalanced force causes movement. The speed of an object is the distance it moves in a certain amount of time. When an object increases its speed, it **accelerates**.

Newton's three laws

Newton's first law: an object will stay still or keep moving steadily in a straight line unless an unbalanced force acts upon it.

ball

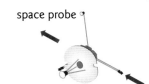
space probe

Newton's second law: different sizes of forces produce different changes in an object's speed or in the direction it moves.

Newton's third law: when a force acts in one direction, another force acts in the opposite direction.

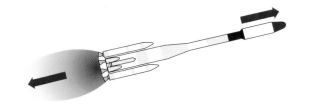

When you are doing nothing

When you sit still, the downward force of your **weight** on the chair is balanced by the upward force of the chair and ground beneath it. By sitting still in your chair, you are following part of Newton's first law of motion, which states that a body will stay still unless it is acted upon by an unbalanced force. Following the same law of motion, your body will start to move when an unbalanced force acts on it. That force will probably be generated by your muscles when you decide to move or get up, although you could also be pulled or pushed out of the chair by someone else!

Making a move

When you prepare to rise from your chair, some of the muscles at the front of your body contract and pull on the upper part of your body. The muscles in your back relax and do not pull in the opposite direction. The unbalanced force makes you rock forward. More unbalanced forces pulling on your legs and arms raise you from your chair.

*A*cceleration

The distance a moving object covers in a certain amount of time is called its speed. When an object begins to move or increase its speed, it is said to accelerate. A force pushes it forward. If you raced in a motorcycle race, you would keep increasing the size of the forward force as you raced down the track. You would be following Newton's second law of motion. By increasing the force on your motorcycle, you would be making it increase its speed or accelerate. If you could make your motorcycle accelerate better than your competitor, you would win the race.

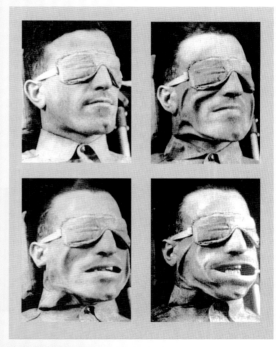

► This test pilot shows how strong forces push on the face during rapid acceleration as in a spacecraft launch. When the acceleration decreases, the forces weaken and his face returns to normal.

◄ The forward force generated by these bikes' engines makes them accelerate down the track.

Speed

As you run along at a steady pace, you cover a certain number of feet every second. This distance per second is called your speed. The speed of something can be measured in other units besides feet per second. A common unit for measuring speed is miles per hour.

Measuring speed

The speed of an object is the measure of how long it takes to travel a certain distance. The object has to be moving steadily before the measurement can be made. When you run a 100-yard race, you **accelerate** away from the start and then run as fast as you can. The time you take to cover this distance is not your speed because for part of the race, you were accelerating.

To measure your speed over 100 yards, you should be running as fast as you can when you pass the starting line and keep running just as fast until you pass the finish line. In the same way, when a speed record is being attempted by a car or boat, it must be going as fast as it can when it begins the measured distance it has to travel.

Shock waves can be seen blowing dust into the air on either side of the car as it reaches the speed of sound during the Thrust team's attempt at the land speed record.

The fastest thing in the universe

Light travels at about 186,300 miles (300,000 kilometers) per second or 670 million miles (1,080 million kilometers) per hour. Scientists believe that nothing travels faster than light. Light that leaves the sun in the direction of the earth takes eight minutes to get here. The next nearest **star** to the sun is called Proxima Centauri. Light leaving this star takes four years and four months to reach us.

The speed of sound

Sounds are made by energy that moves through the air. The energy moves the air particles and makes them vibrate. These movements make sound energy pass through the air. Sound travels through warm air at about 372 yards (340 meters) per second or 760 miles (1224 kilometers) per hour. But in the cooler air 9 miles (14 kilometers) above the earth, it travels more slowly: only 660 miles (1062 kilometers) an hour.

When cars or aircraft travel at the speed of sound, they make a wave of air pressure called a shock wave. This makes a bang called a sonic boom.

Most aircraft that travel at the speed of sound fly at a high **altitude** to prevent the shock wave from reaching the ground.

The speed of sound is used as a unit of measurement of aircraft speed. This unit is called the Mach number, named after Austrian scientist Ernst Mach, who studied fast-moving objects. An aircraft traveling at the speed of sound is traveling at Mach 1; the Concorde flies at Mach 2—twice the speed of sound. Some military aircraft, such as the Blackbird in the Air Force, can fly faster than Mach 3.

The speed trap

Cars, vans, trucks, and motorcycles are fitted with speedometers. These let the driver know the speed of the vehicle so that they can keep within the relevant speed limit. The speed of traffic is checked by police who use a radar gun. The gun is pointed at a vehicle approaching the police officer and **radio waves** are fired. They travel through the air and strike the front of the approaching vehicle. The waves are reflected on the front of the vehicle and travel back to the gun where they are detected by a receiver. The time difference between sending the waves and receiving the reflected waves is used to measure the speed of any vehicle that was targeted by the gun.

▲ Speed traps are often set up on roads where motorists are tempted to break the speed limit.

Friction

You may think that the covers of this book are very smooth, but if you examined them under a microscope, you would see that they are covered in tiny bumps or projections. Other surfaces that you might think are smooth, such as a polished table top, have microscopic bumps too. When two objects touch, the bumps on their surfaces stick together. If there is a push or pull on one of the objects in contact, the bumps that are stuck together resist these **forces** with a force called **friction**.

Two kinds of friction

If you put this book on a table and push the book very gently from one side, the book will stay in its place. The frictional force is strong enough to prevent its movement. This frictional force is called static friction, from the Greek word *stasis* meaning "stillness." The frictional force is pushing in the opposite direction, and it balances the force you are exerting on the book. This follows Newton's third law of motion, which states that when a force is exerted in one direction, a second force of equal size is exerted in the opposite direction.

If you push the book a little harder, some of the bumps no longer stick to each other and the book starts to move. Even at that moment, there are a few bumps sticking together and a force called sliding friction is exerted against your pushing force. The force of this friction does not balance the one you are exerting however, and the book moves.

Moving forever

In space, there is no friction to slow down a moving object. Once the object is given a push, it will keep going. This is stated in Newton's first law of motion. The moving object will not change speed, just as a stationary object on Earth will not move unless given a strong push. In 1971, a **space probe** called Pioneer 10 was launched from Earth. Today it is beyond the edge of the **solar system** and is traveling at 9 miles (14 kilometers) per second. But even at this speed, it will take over 80,000 years to reach another **star**.

Decreasing friction

If you push a heavy box across the floor, the force of friction between the box and the floor is great and the box is difficult to move. This force can be reduced by putting rollers under the box or putting the box on wheels. The rolling action of the wheels and rollers reduces friction and makes the box much easier to move.

Wax is a substance that is rubbed onto a surface to make it very smooth. The wax covers the bumps and stops them from sticking to bumps on other surfaces.

When a liquid flows between two surfaces that are in contact, it moves some of the bumps apart. This reduces the number of bumps on the surfaces sticking together and makes the static and sliding frictional forces smaller.

Oil is used to reduce the friction between the moving parts in a car engine. It makes the engine run smoothly and stops the metal parts from wearing out.

Skiers wax their skis to reduce the friction between the skis and the snow so that they can travel faster.

Increasing friction

The soles of hiking boots have rough surfaces (a deep tread) to help increase friction and help you walk safely over various surfaces.

The tread of a tire is designed to remove water from the surface of a wet road. It helps the surface of the tire and the road to meet so that friction can help the car grip the road and reduce the chance of skidding as the car slows down.

Hiking boots have a deep tread to increase the friction when they touch other surfaces. The friction between the boots and the ground prevents the hiker from slipping.

Air Resistance

Air is made up of tiny particles called atoms and molecules. They move freely and push on any surface that they touch. When an object moves through the air, the particles push against it. This pushing **force** is called **air resistance**. It slows down moving objects in the same way that **friction** does.

Feeling air resistance

If you keep your body low when you quickly pedal a bicycle, you will begin to speed up. If you then sit up, you will feel the push of air resistance on your face and body and you will begin to slow down.

The effect of streamlining

Air resistance can be reduced by making the shape of the moving object streamlined. A streamlined shape has curved surfaces over which the air particles can pass without pushing strongly. Cars are often designed with a streamlined shape. This means they are low at the front and high at the back like a wedge. This wedge shape cuts through the air more easily than the block shape of a truck.

This cyclist has reduced air resistance by crouching low and by wearing a streamlined helmet and tight clothes to give her body a smooth surface.

Diving through the sky

When **sky divers** jump out of an airplane, the pull of Earth's gravity acts on their bodies all the way to the ground. At first, this pull causes the sky divers' bodies to **accelerate** and they fall faster and faster to Earth.

But as they fall, air resistance on their bodies increases and stops them from accelerating. When this happens, the sky divers fall at a steady speed called the terminal velocity, which is about 200 feet (61 meters) per second.

Making a safe landing

If a sky diver hit the ground at 200 feet (61 meters) per second, it would be the same as if he were traveling in a very fast racing car and hit a wall at 250 miles (402 kilometers) per hour. He would be killed instantly. Sky divers make sure that this does not happen by opening their parachutes when they are still far above the earth. The parachute canopy has a very large surface, which is open to the air particles through which it rushes. The particles push up on the canopy and slow it down so that the diver can land without breaking a bone or spraining a joint.

In the rainforests of Southeast Asia, some animals have built-in parachutes. The flying squirrel has folds of skin along its sides that are also connected to its legs. When the squirrel jumps between trees, it stretches out its legs and the folds form a parachute.

▶ When these parachutes were opened, the increase in air resistance slowed down the falling sky divers.

Going Up, Going Down

A life boat is lowered down onto the sea and hits the water with a great splash, but it does not sink. A submarine slowly sinks beneath the waves to rise again hundreds of miles away. A hot air balloon can rise high into the cold evening sky and descend later. These up and down movements are due to the way two **forces** oppose each other. The forces are **weight** and **upthrust**.

Why does a boat float?

When a boat is launched, it pushes a volume of water out of the way to make room for the part of the hull that is below the water surface.
The water that has been pushed out of the way by the hull pushes back on the hull with a force called upthrust. If the upthrust is greater than the weight of the boat pushing down on the water, the boat floats. If the weight of the boat is greater than the upthrust, the boat sinks.

The upthrust of the sea water pushes on this tug boat and keeps it afloat.

How does a submarine sink and rise?

A submarine is equipped with **ballast tanks**. When the submarine is floating at the surface, its ballast tanks are filled with air. At this time, the upthrust is greater than the submarine's weight.

To get a submarine to dive, the crew fills the ballast tanks with water. The water increases the weight of the submarine, so that it is greater than the upthrust.

Later, when the crew needs to get the submarine to rise, compressed air is used to push water out of the ballast tanks. This makes the upthrust greater than the weight of the submarine and the submarine rises toward the surface.

Why don't we float in the air?

Upthrust force is produced by gases as well as liquids. Every object in air has an upthrust pushing on it. Your body pushes a volume of air out of the way to make a space for you to occupy.

The air you displace pushes back on you with a force of about 0.7 **newtons**. This is too small to balance the force of your weight, which may be from 350–490 newtons.

The rise and fall of a hot air balloon

When air inside a hot air balloon is heated, the air **expands**. Some of the air passes out of the bottom of the balloon. The air remaining in the balloon has a smaller weight than the upthrust of the air around the balloon. This difference between the weight of the air in the balloon and the upthrust around it makes the balloon rise into the sky.

When the air in the balloon is allowed to cool down, it **contracts** and more air is drawn in. The weight of the air in the balloon increases. When the weight is greater than the upthrust, the balloon sinks to the ground.

► Upthrust around these balloons raises them hundreds of feet into the sky.

Pressure

If someone pokes your arm, you feel a pushing **force** over an area of your skin. When a force acts over an area in this way, pressure is created.

Cleats and spikes

When you stand up, you are in contact with the ground through the soles of your feet. Your feet cover an area of the ground and your body **weight** pushing down on the ground is spread out over this area. The pressure on the ground is not great enough for you to sink into the turf of a playing field. If you were to play a sport such as soccer or football on grass in ordinary shoes, your shoes would press down without breaking through the turf, and you might slip if the grass was wet.

Shoes and boots used for playing sports on grass have cleats. When you wear them, your weight presses down on a smaller area—the tips of the cleats—and the pressure on the ground in those smaller areas is much greater. This increase in pressure pushes the cleats into the turf so that your feet grip the playing field without slipping.

Pressure is due to a force acting over an area. Increasing pressure by using cleats helps sports players grip the playing field. Pressure helps skaters move. Reducing pressure can help people walk on snow or drink through a straw.

When you skate on ice

Ice is an unusual solid. When it is squeezed very, very hard, it turns into a liquid—water.

The blade on an ice skate concentrates your weight onto a small area on the ice. When you set off across the ice, the pressure of your weight on the ice beneath the blade makes the ice melt. This means that when you skate, you actually slide along on a **film** of water. As you move on and no longer press down on the ice, it freezes again behind you.

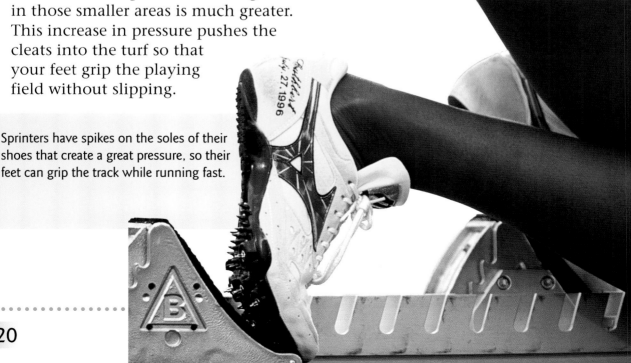

Sprinters have spikes on the soles of their shoes that create a great pressure, so their feet can grip the track while running fast.

Snow walking

When you stand on snow, it pushes against the pressure of your feet. The pushing force of the snow is weaker than your weight and you may sink up to your knees in it! People who have to walk through snow wear snowshoes, which are like tennis rackets strapped to their feet. The large area of the snowshoe reduces the pressure of your body on the snow so that it matches the upward pushing force of the snow, and you do not sink.

► These snow shoes prevent the wearer from sinking into the snow.

Air pressure

Air exerts a pressure all around us. You use air pressure to drink through a straw. When you suck on a straw, you remove air from it, and air can no longer push down on the drink inside the straw. The air pressure pushing down on the rest of the liquid surface pushes the drink into your mouth.

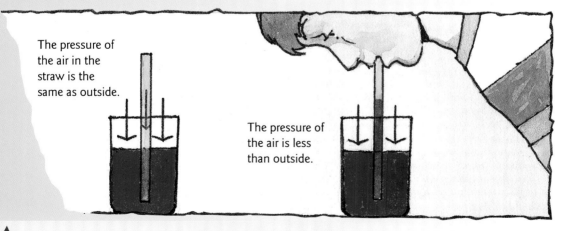

The pressure of the air in the straw is the same as outside.

The pressure of the air is less than outside.

▲ When the air pressure in the straw falls, the level of the drink rises.

Machines

We tend to think of machines as large, noisy devices, yet most machines are much smaller and quieter than this. A machine is a device that makes a task easier to do. It does this by increasing the size of a **force**, changing the direction of a force, or increasing the movement produced by a force.

SCIENCE ESSENTIALS

A machine makes work easier. It increases the size of a force, changes the force's direction, or increases the movement a force produces. A **lever** is a simple machine. There are three types of levers. They vary in the position of the **pivot** and the places where the forces act. A "moment of a force" is a turning effect the force produces.

The door machine

When you push down on a door handle, you exert a force on it. The pivot on which the handle turns is inside the handle. A short bar that pushes against a strong spring to release the door catch is on the other side of the pivot. The handle, pivot, and bar make up a simple machine called a lever. The lever increases your small pushing force on the handle into a large pushing force on the spring so that you can open the door easily.

Types of levers

The lever is one of the simplest machines that exists. There are three types or classes of lever. The force applied to them is called the **effort force**, and the force they produce is called the **load force**. The places where the effort force and load force are applied are different in each type of lever, as the diagram below shows.

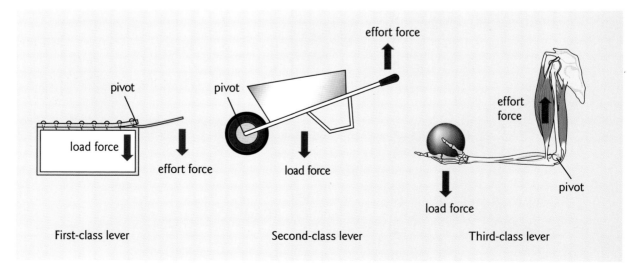

First-class lever   Second-class lever   Third-class lever

Multipliers and magnifiers

In a first-class or second-class lever, the effort force moves over a long distance and produces a larger load force that moves over a short distance. These classes of levers are called force multipliers.

▶ These machines are being assembled from smaller parts called components. Many of the components are simple machines like levers. The components work together to make a larger machine that performs a special task like washing clothes.

In a third-class lever, the large effort force moves over a short distance and produces a smaller force that moves over a longer distance. This class of lever is called a distance magnifier.

Just a moment

Although a force acts in a straight line, it can produce a turning movement. The turning effect is called the moment of a force. For example, when a wrench is used to release a nut, a clockwise moment may be produced. The moment of a force not only depends on the strength of the force, but also on the distance of the force from the pivot. On a seesaw, the pivot is in the middle. The moments of the forces pushing down on one side of the seesaw's beam are clockwise, while the moments of the forces on the other side of the beam are counterclockwise. If two people of the same weight sit at the same distance on either side of the pivot, the two moments are the same and the seesaw balances. If one person moves closer or further away from the pivot, the seesaw tips because the moments are no longer balanced.

◀ This mechanic is applying turning movements with the wrenches to tighten the nuts on this car.

Magnetic Forces

Magnets are fascinating because they exert forces on magnetic materials without touching them. The size of a magnetic force is strongest close to the magnet and gets weaker as the distance from the magnet increases.

The first magnets were discovered more than two thousand years ago. They were black rocks containing iron, which were named magnetite. The country where they were found was called Magnesia, which is now part of Turkey.

Magnetic materials

A magnetic material is made from one or more of four metals—iron, steel, cobalt, and nickel. It can be made into a magnet that will exert a magnetic force on other magnetic materials. Some materials such as paper, wood, and pottery are not affected by magnetic forces. A magnetic force can pass through this type of nonmagnetic material and act on magnetic material on the other side. For example, a magnet on the front of a refrigerator door can hold note paper and post cards in place because its magnetic force pulls it close to the steel door.

The magnetic field

A magnet exerts a magnetic force in the space around it. The force is strongest close to the **magnetic poles** (at each end) and weaker further away. The space around a magnet in which the magnetic force acts is called the magnetic field. When a magnetic material enters a magnetic field, a magnetic force acts on it.

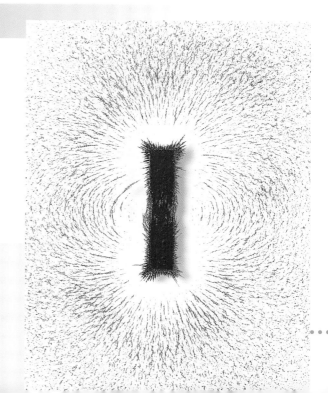

▶ If iron filings are sprinkled on paper and a magnet is placed on the sheet, the magnetic forces pull the filings into lines around the magnet. These lines of force show how far the force field extends around the magnet.

Pointing north and south

If a magnet is hung from a thread, it will swing around and then settle with one end pointing north and the other end pointing south. The end pointing north contains the north-seeking pole of the magnet. The end pointing south contains the south-seeking pole. The magnet lines up this way because the inside of the earth generates a magnetic field. The field seems as if it is produced by a huge bar magnet inside the earth, but it is believed to be caused by the way iron and nickel move at the earth's core as the planet spins.

The pushing, pulling poles

If two magnets are brought together with their north-seeking poles (or their south-seeking poles) facing each other, they will push each other apart. The like poles repel each other. If one magnet is turned around so that the north-seeking and south-seeking poles are together, the magnets will attract each other. Opposite poles attract each other.

Electricity and magnetism

When a current of electricity flows through a wire, it creates a magnetic field. If the wire is made into a coil, it behaves like a magnet when electricity passes through it. A magnet made in this way is called an electromagnet and is used in devices such as door bells and **security locks** on doors.

Levitation

This monorail train in Sydney, Australia, is a maglev train. This type of train uses electromagnets to make it move. There are electromagnets in both the train and the track. As the train moves along, electricity is passed through the train's electromagnets. The electromagnets on the track repel those on the train. This **repulsion** makes the train rise and **levitate** above the track. A second set of electromagnets on the track and train attract each other to pull the train along.

The Electric Motor

The electric motor was invented following the study of how **magnets** and wires carrying electricity push and pull on each other. There are two magnets in an electric motor. One is a permanent magnet, and the other is an **electromagnet**. The movement produced in the electric motor is caused by the pushing and pulling **forces** that the two magnets exert on each other.

SCIENCE ESSENTIALS

An electric motor contains a permanent magnet and an electromagnet. Magnetic forces between the two magnets make the motor produce a turning action. Electric motors have many uses.

The magnetic sandwich

In an electric motor, the coil of wire is sandwiched between the north and south poles of the permanent magnet. The coil is attached to a rod and can spin around. When the coil spins, the rod spins too. The spinning end of the rod can be connected to other parts of a machine to make a useful force that will spin a wheel or turntable.

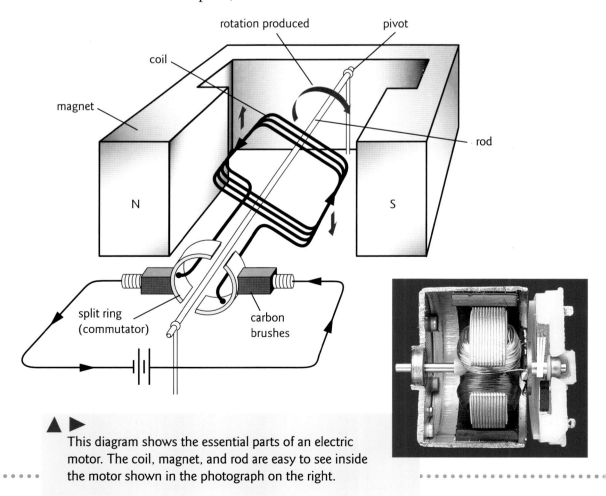

▲ ▶
This diagram shows the essential parts of an electric motor. The coil, magnet, and rod are easy to see inside the motor shown in the photograph on the right.

Switch on . . .

In a motor, the ends of the wire in the coil are attached into an electric circuit by a device called a **commutator**. When the current is switched on, the electricity flows in one direction through the commutator and the coil. This makes the coil into an electromagnet. The north (and south) poles of the electromagnet are attracted to the south (and north) poles of the permanent magnet. These forces of attraction make the coil turn.

When the opposite poles face each other, the commutator switches the direction of the current through the coil. This reverses the poles of the electromagnet and they are repelled by the poles of the permanent magnet. The forces of repulsion make the coil move again. As the electromagnet's poles keep changing, they push and pull on the poles of the permanent magnet and keep the rod spinning.

Motors at work and in your home

When you dry your hair with a hair dryer or brush your teeth with an electric toothbrush, you are using an electric motor. A motor spins a compact disc or pulls the tape in an audio or videocassette. A motor provides the power to circulate the coolant in a refrigerator to keep your food fresh, and turns the beaters in a food mixer.

The turntable in a microwave oven is spun by an electric motor and your clothes are washed as they are tumbled by an electric motor in a washing machine.

This locomotive picks up the electric current from an overhead cable through the metal structure called a **pantograph** on the locomotive's roof. The huge electric motor in the locomotive produces a force strong enough to pull a train weighing hundreds of tons.

Time to Stop

When a moving object slows down, it is said to **decelerate**. If the object is allowed to continue decelerating, it will eventually stop.

The push of friction

If you kick a ball, it rolls along the ground. **Friction** acts on the parts of the ball that touch the ground. This **force** pushes in the opposite direction of the way the ball is rolling. If the ball does not receive another kick, it continues to decelerate and then stops.

The tired arrow

People in ancient times used to think that when an arrow was shot from a bow, the air that was pushed out of the way by the arrow rushed to the back of it and pushed it forward. They believed that the arrow slowed down and fell to the ground when the air was tired of pushing it. They did not know that the arrow fell because of the force of **gravity** and decelerated because of the push of **air resistance**.

Putting on the brakes

Almost every vehicle with wheels is fitted with **brakes**. The brakes are made from blocks or pads of tough material that can be pushed against a part of the wheel. On a bicycle, the brake blocks push against the wheel rim; on a car, there are pads that press on a disk around the wheel hub. Brakes are operated by **levers** like those on a bicycle's handlebars or a pedal in a car.

When someone puts on the brakes, the blocks or pads are pressed onto the wheel so that friction is increased and the bicycle or car decelerates.

▼
To turn corners, race car drivers have to slow down their cars within seconds. If they slam on their brakes too hard, they skid off the track.

Slowing down safely

A driver cannot stop a vehicle immediately. First the driver has to think about stopping. During this time, the vehicle continues at its normal speed. The distance covered by the vehicle in this time is called the thinking distance.

When the driver has thought about stopping, the brakes are then applied, causing the vehicle to decelerate and eventually stop. The distance covered by the vehicle while it slows down, until it stops, is called the braking distance. These two distances are added together to make the total stopping distance. For example, a car traveling at 30 miles (48 kilometers) per hour travels 30 feet (9 meters) while the driver thinks about braking and 46 feet (14 meters) while the driver applies the brakes—a total stopping distance of 76 feet (23 meters). These distances increase as the car goes faster or if it travels on a wet road.

SCIENCE ESSENTIALS

When a moving object slows down it decelerates.
Air resistance and friction slow down moving objects.
Brakes increase friction on a wheel.

Exploring space safely

By studying the laws of forces and **motion,** we have devised many ways to start objects moving, control their speed, and stop them safely. However, we live on an object—the earth—that does not have any brakes. It is pulled around the sun by the force of gravity. All the other objects in the **solar system** are also moved by gravitational forces and can only be stopped when they collide into something else. If you look at a full **moon** through a telescope, you can see craters where large chunks of rock have crashed into its surface long ago when the solar system was forming.

In spite of the problems of gravitational forces, we are able to construct **space probes** that can reach and explore other planets. We apply our knowledge of forces and motion in the planning and construction of these spacecraft so that they will travel safely through space and land on other worlds.

This is an artist's impression of how a space probe will land on another planet.

29

Glossary

accelerate   increase in speed

air resistance   push of air on a moving object

altitude   height

ballast tank   container on a submarine that is used to hold air or water

black hole   region of space that has such a strong gravitational field that not even light can escape from it

brake   device to make a vehicle slow down and stop

commutator   device that allows electricity to reach the coil in an electric motor

contract   become smaller and occupy less space

decelerate   decrease in speed

effort force   force applied to a lever to oppose a load force and create movement

electromagnet   device that becomes a magnet when electricity passes through it

energy   ability to make something happen

expand   increase in size and occupy more space

film   thin layer of a substance

force   push or pull that can change the movement of the shape of an object

friction   force that exists between two objects that are touching when a pushing force is applied to one object

galaxy   large group of stars

gravitational field   region around a large object, such as a planet, where its gravity pulls on other objects around it

gravity   force of attraction that exists between any two objects in the universe

lever   simple machine that enables a small force to produce a large amount of work

levitate   rise above ground and float at a certain distance above it

load force   force executed by an object on a lever that can be overcome by the application of an effort force

magnet   metal object that can attract and repel other magnets and can attract unmagnetized metals such as iron and steel

magnetic pole   region in a magnet where the magnetic force is very strong

mass   amount of matter in an object or a substance such as water or air

Milky Way   the galaxy that contains the solar system

moon   rocky object that moves around a planet

motion   process in which an object changes position

newton   unit used for measuring forces

orbit   path of a planet or comet around a star, or a moon around a planet

pantograph   device on a locomotive with an electric motor for collecting electricity from overhead cables

pivot   place or object on which something turns

pulse   movement of a particular type of blood vessel (called an artery), caused by the action of the heart

radar (short for **ra**dio **d**etection **a**nd **r**anging) system that uses radio waves and their reflections to detect objects

radio waves waves that have electrical and magnetic properties, such as light waves and microwaves

repulsion pushing apart of two objects, usually due to a magnetic force

security lock lock on a door that is opened by pressing buttons on it in a particular sequence, rather than by using a key. These locks often contain electromagnets.

shock wave wave of air of a different pressure than the surrounding air. Shock waves travel away from a fast-moving object.

sky diver person who falls a long way through the air for pleasure before opening his or her parachute

solar system the sun and its orbiting planets, moons, and comets

space probe device used to investigate objects in the solar system and beyond

star huge ball of gas in which hydrogen gas changes to helium gas with the release of light and heat

streamlined shape shape that passes easily through air or water

submarine vessel that can travel underwater. It is used for military purposes and may carry missiles and torpedoes and can stay underwater for weeks. Small submarines that can only stay under water for short periods are called submersibles and are used for exploring the ocean.

terminal velocity steady speed at which an object falls when the forces of gravity and air resistance are equal

tide rise and fall of the sea level

universe all space and everything in it, including stars and planets

upthrust the upward force on an object that comes from the liquid or gas surrounding it

wax solid material made from chemicals in oil

weight force with which an object pushes downward on a planet or moon

More Books to Read

Bardon, Keith. *Forces & Structures*. Austin, Tex.: Raintree Steck-Vaughn, 1992.

Gardner, Robert. *Experiments with Motion*. Springfield, N.J.: Enslow Publishers, Incorporated, 1995.

Kerrod, Robin. *Force & Motion*. Tarrytown, N.Y.: Cavendish, Marshall Corporation, 1993.

Sauvain, Philip. *Motion*. Old Tappan, N.J.: Simon & Schuster Children's, 1992.

Index